BASIC.WHO IS GOD?
FOLLOWER'S GUIDE

FRANCIS CHAN
with Mark Beuving

David C Cook®
transforming lives together

WHO IS GOD? FOLLOWER'S GUIDE
Published by David C Cook
4050 Lee Vance View
Colorado Springs, CO 80918 U.S.A.

David C Cook Distribution Canada
55 Woodslee Avenue, Paris, Ontario, Canada N3L 3E5

David C Cook U.K., Kingsway Communications
Eastbourne, East Sussex BN23 6NT, England

David C Cook and the graphic circle C logo
are registered trademarks of Cook Communications Ministries.

ISBN 978-1-4347-0085-8
eISBN 978-1-4347-0292-0

Printed in the United States of America
First Edition 2010

1 2 3 4 5 6 7 8 9 10

091510

Contents

INTRODUCTION

Welcome to the BASIC.WHO IS GOD? *Follower's Guide.* This workbook is designed to help you think through the material that you will be watching in the WHO IS GOD? films and then discussing as a group. I'm sure that you'll be challenged as you watch the three films (FEAR GOD, FOLLOW JESUS, and HOLY SPIRIT). And I'm confident that your small-group discussions will help you process the material in those films. But if you stop with those two things, I think you'll miss out.

That's why we've included this *Follower's Guide.* As challenging as the films are, I'm afraid that once the reality of everyday life sets in, the conviction you feel will be drowned out by a tidal wave of distractions. This workbook offers you the opportunity to take what you've seen in the films and what you've discussed with your small group and sit with it. My prayer is that you will approach each of the seven sessions in this workbook patiently and prayerfully.

A *Follower's Guide* like this isn't effective unless you're prepared to examine your heart and open up your life to the truth of God's Word. You could read through each of the sessions in just a few minutes, but I hope you won't move that quickly. I've built in times for prayer, thoughtful meditation, and Bible study. The more you allow the material to soak in, the more you'll get out of this process. I challenge you to meditate on the Scripture presented, honestly examine your heart, and push yourself to apply what you're studying to your everyday life.

The material in these sessions will lead you to think about who God is. We all have ideas about God, but those ideas are often formed more by our own experiences with the Christian life than by the way God describes Himself. My prayer is that you will see God for who He truly is and that your life will be changed as a result.

The BASIC Process

For each of the three films included in the BASIC.WHO IS GOD? Small Group Experience box set, we've created two *Follower's Guide* sessions for individual study, along with a seventh session at the end to help you put into practice what you've explored. So once you've discussed each BASIC.WHO IS GOD? session with your small group, use this *Follower's Guide* on your own to go deeper into that topic. The sessions in this *Follower's Guide* are designed to be worked through *after* you've watched the corresponding BASIC film and discussed the corresponding small-group session, which are on the BASIC.WHO IS GOD? DVDs.

So the process for getting the most out of the BASIC.WHO IS GOD? Small Group Experience goes like this:

1. You view the film FEAR GOD with your small group.

2. On the FEAR GOD disc, return to the top menu and select "Session 1." Question 1 will appear on your screen. Discuss

that question, then click [Next] for question 2, and so on until
the end of the discussion.

3. Make sure each person in the group has a copy of this *Follower's
Guide*. After your discussion of Session 1 on the DVD, go
home and take about an hour on your own to think and pray
through the questions for FEAR GOD Session 1 in this guide.
Write notes in the space provided. This is your chance to decide
if you are truly on board with what God is saying to you in
FEAR GOD.

4. Gather with your group for your next discussion. On the FEAR
GOD DVD menu screen, select "Session 2." Discuss each
question in turn. Session 2 includes clips from the film, so you
don't have to view the entire film again if you choose not to. If
you prefer, though, you can always view the whole film again.

5. After your group sessions ends, take some time on your own
in the following week to think and pray through FEAR GOD
Session 2 in this *Follower's Guide*.

6. Repeat this same process for FOLLOW JESUS and HOLY
SPIRIT. The HOLY SPIRIT disc also includes a seventh discussion session called "BASIC.LIVING."

7. Lastly, think and pray through the BASIC.LIVING session in
this *Follower's Guide*.

If you're leading a discussion group through BASIC.WHO IS GOD? check out the Tips for Leaders at the end of this guide. (The Extras DVD also has a downloadable PDF of the Tips for Leaders section.)

1

FEAR GOD

FEAR GOD
Session 1

Every person who comes into contact with God falls to the ground in fear. Maybe that statement surprises you a bit. We have become so familiar with the thought of God that many people can't imagine being afraid in God's presence. It's not uncommon to hear someone say, "When I get to heaven, the first thing I'm going to do is ask God why _____." And while the thought of having all of our questions answered is appealing, I think these statements reveal an overly casual view of God.

Personally, it makes perfect sense to me that we should be terrified in God's presence. The thought of coming face-to-face with an infinite, holy, all-powerful, all-knowing Being is disconcerting to say the least. But how often do we actually think of God like this? For most of us, it is difficult to consistently see God for who He truly is. And I think that's why we have a difficult time understanding the fear of the Lord.

On rare occasions, people in the Bible found themselves standing before

God. They were going about their lives as usual, and then suddenly they were in the presence of unlimited power, of pure holiness. They didn't have to think about what it means to fear the Lord—they were absolutely terrified and fell on their faces as if they were dead. They didn't have to conjure up a feeling of fear, because fear is the natural response to God.

But we rarely see this type of fear in the church today. There are probably some good intentions behind this: It is important to understand God's love for the world and to view God as a caring Father—but in many cases, I'm afraid that we either don't understand who God is or, worse yet, we're embarrassed by some of His attributes.

Perhaps you've never really thought about fearing God. Or maybe you're a person who actually strives to understand and live with a healthy fear of God. Either way, God is who He is, and it is absolutely essential for us to come to God for who He is, not for who we'd like Him to be.

Psalm 111:10 says, "The fear of the Lord is the beginning of wisdom." There are many things that we could and even should study about God, but the fear of the Lord is foundational. The psalmist tells us that we can't even *begin* to live wisely until we come to a place of fearing God.

1. Why do you think the psalmist calls the fear of the Lord "the beginning of wisdom"?

Though the fear of the Lord is foundational, finding Christians who obviously fear God is the exception, not the norm. I think we've downplayed God's power and greatness on a broad scale for a long time. But rather than trying to correct the problem generally, let's start with you personally. Think about your own life. Consider the way you view God, and then answer the following questions.

2. As you examine your life, do you actually fear God? What evidence is there that you do or don't fear God?

3. We all have basic assumptions about God. Some of these are scripturally based; many are not. Try to honestly assess your view of God. Jot down a brief description of some of the ways you view God, and give a short explanation of why you've come to see God in these ways. (For example, "I picture God as patient and forgiving because my father is very kind.")

4. As we talk about God being terrifying, all-powerful, and in charge, what is your natural response? Don't think about how you'd like to respond; instead, tune in to the mental pictures, emotions, and bodily reactions that stir within you as you think about these things. How do these thoughts strike you? (For example, do you find yourself tensing up? Feeling peaceful? Growing defiant? Picturing God in a specific way? Remembering a scary person in your past?)

5. While we can't change God, it is helpful to tune in to our reaction to Him. What do your natural responses tell you about your view of and relationship with God?

Regardless of the degree to which we do or don't fear God, the people in the Bible who encountered God were terrified. A great example of this was the apostle John. Late in his life, John was sent to an island called Patmos as an exile because he was a follower of Christ. While on this island, he received a vision and saw the resurrected Jesus in all of His glory.

Read Revelation 1:9–18 slowly and carefully. We can be so quick to read right past important details. Try to get the feel of what John was experiencing. Throughout the book of Revelation, I get the impression that John is struggling to capture in human language a full sense of what he is seeing, hearing, and feeling. Yet his language is vivid. Allow yourself to experience this scene along with John. After you've spent some time reading and meditating on the passage, answer the following questions thoughtfully.

6. Try to picture what John was seeing. How does he describe his vision of Jesus?

7. Try to place yourself in John's shoes. Jesus suddenly appears before you as described in Revelation 1. How do you respond? What goes through your mind? (Try to be descriptive.)

While it's helpful to learn from John's experience with God, at some point you need to experience Him yourself. Granted, visions and face-to-face encounters are rare, both in the Bible and in our everyday lives, but we can't get around the fact that this Jesus who moved John to fall on his face is the same Jesus we worship, pray to, and love. Just because God has not allowed you to see Him in His full glory does not mean that you shouldn't fear Him. This is a part of what it means to walk by faith, not by sight. I have never seen God as Isaiah or John did, but I am absolutely certain that God is someone I should fear.

8. Take some time to consider your relationship with God. As you read these words, this all-powerful God is with you, right now. Rather than imagining what it would have been like for Isaiah or John to be in God's presence, meditate on the fact that you are in His presence right now. Spend ten to fifteen minutes in prayer as you immerse yourself in the reality of God's presence. Be careful not to revert to a more comfortable image of God at this point—see yourself in the presence of the fear-inspiring God who showed Himself to Isaiah and John. Talk with Him about what it's like to be in His presence. Don't worry about what you think you ought to feel—this time of openness and honesty before God is invaluable. Write down any notes from your prayer

9. After spending some time meditating on God's presence, write down a
few thoughts. How does this understanding make you feel? How does it
change the way you view God?

When John encountered Jesus, his vision was startling—he turned around
and saw Jesus with bright white hair, fiery eyes, glowing skin, thundering
voice, swordlike tongue, and face shining like the sun. I'm not surprised that
John fell at his feet like a dead man. What surprises me is Jesus' response.
I don't know what I would expect Jesus to say in a situation like this, but I
certainly wouldn't expect Him to say, "Fear not."

Not until we come to grips with the fearful reality of who God truly is
can we understand the security that comes from belonging to Him. In the
next session, we will begin considering the impact of hearing Jesus' reassuring
voice telling us to "Fear not." In the meantime, push yourself to maintain
a strong sense of the fear of the Lord, and watch for ways that this fear can
affect your daily thoughts and actions.

Note: If you come from a traumatic background, such as growing up with an abusive parent, you may struggle when it comes to the principle of fearing God. You may have transferred some images onto God that don't belong to Him, our perfect Father. Now you need to hear the good news of session 2: God is scary but not abusive. This all-powerful God loves you without using you. God isn't tame, but He is trustworthy, and He says, "Fear not." God deals with each of us uniquely, and learning to fear Him will look different for those who have been abused.

If you come from trauma and you're inclined to panic or run away from the Jesus of Revelation 1, find someone to talk to about this. God's ultimate goal is to heal your heart so that you can embrace this Jesus. Healing takes time, and often the help of a mature believer who can bear your burden can keep you grounded in the Word.

FEAR GOD
Session 2

The fear of the Lord leads to life. We all naturally pursue life and happiness, but who would think to start with fear? Initially, fearing God seems like it would make us unhappy and lead us away from life. After all, the fear of the Lord led John to fall on his face like a dead man. When we talk about fearing God, things can get emotional, but happiness is one emotion that usually doesn't come into play. And I think that's why the fear of the Lord has become so unpopular. We are a people who want to "think happy thoughts."

But what do we do with a statement like Proverbs 19:23 (NASB): "The fear of the LORD leads to life, so that one may sleep satisfied, untouched by evil"? We are prone to pursue life and satisfaction by avoiding fear, but Solomon tells us that fear is actually the place to begin. When we encounter God, we can't help but fall over in fear. But God is the source of life and satisfaction, and until we come to God as He is, we will never find what we're looking for.

Consider the apostle John. We've already read of his encounter with the risen Jesus in Revelation 1. While in exile on a small island, he heard a voice behind him. As he turned to see who was speaking, he saw Jesus in all of His resurrected glory. His hair was bright white, His eyes were aflame, His voice roared like the ocean, His open mouth produced a sharp two-edged sword, and looking into His face was like staring at the sun. John's response was simple: "When I saw him, I fell at his feet as though dead" (Revelation 1:17).

Though John's encounter is much different from the way most people typically think about Jesus, this was reality. In an instant, all of John's speculations about what it would be like to see Jesus again became irrelevant. There was no time to think about how one ought to respond to Jesus—no chance to find answers to life's nagging questions—there was just Jesus. And having seen Him for who He truly is, John fell at His feet like a dead man.

In the last session of this guide we considered what it would be like to stand in John's shoes. This is an important step in coming to terms with Jesus-as-He-is, rather than Jesus-as-I'd-like-Him-to-be. We can't pick and choose aspects of Jesus that fit our needs and agendas. He is who He is. And just like John, we must face reality and come to that place of fear. Only then will we begin to understand who God is.

Once again, read Revelation 1:9–18 slowly and carefully. Try to place yourself in John's shoes—experience what he experienced. Last week we focused on the fear that John felt. This week, however, focus on Jesus' response to John. When John falls over like a dead man, how does Jesus respond? Be careful not to rush this. After you've spent some time reading and meditating on the passage, answer the following questions thoughtfully.

1. It's clear that John found himself in a terrifying situation. So why do you think Jesus told John to "Fear not"?

John rightly understood that he could not stand in Jesus' presence. I don't know what John was thinking when he "fell at his feet as though dead," but I'm certain that what came next was a shock to him. John says it so simply: "But he laid his right hand on me, saying, 'Fear not'" (Revelation 1:17).

2. Place yourself in this moment. You have just seen Jesus in His full glory and have fallen on your face in terror. What is it like to feel Jesus' hand on your body and to hear His reassuring voice say, "Fear not"? (Try to be descriptive. Imagine yourself in the scene. How do you respond emotionally? Physically? Cognitively?)

The fact that this wasn't John's first encounter with Jesus makes this passage even more fascinating. Remember that John was one of Jesus' twelve apostles. He spent three years living closely with Jesus. He was there when Jesus was crucified. He even spent time with Jesus after His resurrection. John was very familiar with Jesus—he went as far as to refer to himself as the "disciple whom Jesus loved." After Jesus ascended into heaven, John remained a devoted follower. In fact, that's why John was on the island of Patmos—he had been sent into exile for ministering on Jesus' behalf.

So when John encountered Jesus, I would picture it being a warm reunion. The fact that John fell on his face shows how overwhelming it is for a human to stand in God's presence. But Jesus' response demonstrates His continued love for John. John couldn't control the fear he felt, but Jesus was reassuring. John was still loved and accepted.

Sometimes we downplay the fear of God because we want to make sure people know that God loves them. We want them to feel secure in their relationships with Him. But why can't God be terrifying and loving all at once? Doesn't the fear of God amplify His great love for us? That's exactly what John experienced. He didn't need Jesus to hide His glory and majesty from him. Jesus showed up, John was terrified, and Jesus gently laid His hand on John and told him not to be afraid.

As counterintuitive as it may seem, when we remake Jesus into a more "palatable" version of Himself, we actually diminish the greatness of His love. We would expect a cuddly Jesus to tell us not to be afraid (though He probably wouldn't need to). But when we hear those same words from the mouth of this all-powerful Jesus whose words are like a two-edged sword, there is a profound difference.

3. Why does it mean more to hear "Fear not" from the real Jesus, rather than a tamer version of Jesus?

4. What is the difference between being loved by a toned-down, lovable Jesus, and being loved by this Jesus who appeared to John in all His glory?

Allow Jesus' words to John to really sink in. After telling him not to be afraid, Jesus said, "I am the first and the last, and the living one. I died, and behold I am alive forevermore, and I have the keys of Death and Hades" (Rev. 1:17–18). Spend some time thinking about what these words mean. John knew that Jesus had died—he witnessed it. These words that Jesus spoke to John must have carried a lot of meaning.

5. Why would the words "I am alive forevermore" have been a huge comfort to John?

6. Though Jesus said these words directly to John, they carry profound meaning for us as well. Spend some time meditating on His words: "Fear

not. I am ... the living one.... I am alive forevermore." What difference should it make to your everyday life that Jesus is alive forevermore?

Until we come to the point of fearing God, our relationship with Him will be superficial and distorted. But once we come to that place of fear, we will find that there is nothing else to fear. Seeing God in all of His power and glory allows us to see beyond ourselves, to see that this life is all about Him. And when we understand that this fear-inducing God loves us unconditionally, all other fears subside. As Paul says, "If God is for us, who can be against us?" (Romans 8:31).

7. What things in your life right now are sources of fear?

8. How does fearing God change the way you view these fears?

Fearing God opens up a new depth in our relationship with Him. This is one of those important truths that serve as a foundation for the Christian life. When I first began to truly fear God, I found that it changed many things about the way I viewed and followed God. We will explore some of those aspects in the weeks ahead.

9. Spend some time in prayer. Take some time to picture Jesus as He appeared to John. Picture Him laying His hand on you and reassuring you that you don't need to be afraid. And then pray to Him. Talk to Him for who He is—high and exalted, yet gentle and loving. Ask Him to continue to use these truths to change the way you think and live.

Note: When we talk about God as a loving Father who defends and protects His children—when we say that there is nothing else to fear—a very important question comes up. The question looks a little different to each of us, but it sounds something like this:

If I have nothing to fear as a child of God, then why did _____ happen to me?

Where was God when I was raped? Why are Christians martyred for their faith? There are answers to these questions, but we simply won't know all of the reasons behind our suffering on this side of eternity. One thing that we can say with confidence is that God often uses horrific events for a greater purpose. The Bible includes many examples of this, in addition to what God still does on a daily basis.

Consider Joseph, for example. His brothers sold him into slavery. From there, he was falsely accused and imprisoned. But God had a greater purpose for Joseph's suffering. From the rock bottom of an Egyptian prison cell, God raised Joseph up to rule over all Egypt. He even used Joseph to preserve human life in the midst of a famine. And when Joseph's brothers apologized for selling him into slavery, Joseph replied without hesitation: "You meant evil against me, but God meant it for good" (Genesis 50:20).

Or consider Job. After all that God allowed him to go through, God never explained Himself. Job simply had to trust that God had greater purposes behind his suffering.

I don't know the reasons behind the intense pain in your life. But I know God is good. I know pain and suffering exist in this world because we have rebelled against God. God created a perfect world, but from the moment that we sinned against Him, this world has been filled with suffering and death. The incredible truth of the gospel is that Jesus died to restore the world to what He intended it to be. As Paul says, "I consider that the sufferings of this present time are not worth comparing with the glory that is to be revealed to us" (Romans 8:18).

Though we will have suffering in this world, we can still look to God as a loving Father. And when we see Him in this way, we really do have nothing to fear. This world still has people and situations that can inflict terrible pain: rape, the death of a child, war, excruciating illness, unemployment, cruelty (to name only a few). Jesus knew that people can and often do harm us physically and emotionally. But He pointed us beyond these things to a deeper reality: "Do not fear those who kill the body but cannot kill the soul. Rather fear him who can destroy both soul and body in hell" (Matthew 10:28). Sometimes it's hard to believe that the things people do to us in this life can't kill the soul, but it's true—they can scar it, but they cannot destroy it.

In preparing His disciples for the suffering that they would soon endure, Jesus said, "You will be delivered up even by parents and brothers and relatives and friends, and some of you they will put to death. You will be hated by all for my name's sake. But not a hair of your head will perish. By your endurance you will gain your lives" (Luke 21:16–19). There is something so beautiful about Jesus saying, *"Not a hair of your head will perish"* in the midst of explaining that some of His followers will be killed. We are not promised health, wealth, or the American Dream, but Jesus loves and cares for us as His children.

These answers can come across as glib or uncaring—but only if we try to use them as quick fixes. Ultimately, these answers don't point us to a method or even a state of mind. Rather, they point us to a Person. They point us to the only Person who truly understands what is happening in this world. Only He has an eternal perspective on what we encounter every day. And that Person is our loving Father, our friend, and our husband who gave up His life for us, His bride. Don't trust an answer; trust God. See Him as the only one to fear, and as the only one who can truly love and care for you in the midst of any and every circumstance.

If you are suffering now, or have suffered in the past, or are facing suffering in the future that causes you to question whether God is really keeping you safe from ultimate harm, take some time to talk with Him about it. Tell Him what has hurt you and what scares you. Talk to the Jesus who has been through profound suffering and death and came out the other side. Talk to the Jesus who claims to hold the keys of death.

FOLLOW JESUS

FOLLOW JESUS
Session 1

In one sense, it doesn't take much to follow the leader. You don't have to put a lot of thought into it. The leader hops on one leg, so you hop on one leg. When the leader stops, you stop. There is a profound simplicity to the whole thing.

But in another sense, it can cost everything to follow the leader. By imitating another person, you're giving up your own plans and desires. So while it's easy to follow someone else, it can also be difficult because you may not want to do what the leader is doing. If you choose to follow someone exactly like you, then the game will be easy. But when you follow someone with different thoughts and priorities, you may not want to play for long. It all depends on who you're following. For the most part, we choose heroes and leaders who are very similar to us. And where there are differences, they are generally minor and desirable (e.g., wealth, fame, charisma). But what do you do when the leader is Jesus?

When we call ourselves Christians, what we're saying is that we are followers of Christ. But how many of us really want to play follow the leader with someone as convicting and socially unacceptable as Jesus? It's not that there aren't aspects of His life that everyone would want to emulate. Everyone believes that love is a good thing. Most people believe in pursuing righteousness. Our society even applauds those who want to care for the poor. But nobody wants to get carried away.

Jesus is too extreme for the average American. We love the people who love us, but who really wants to love their enemies? We want to be considered righteous, but who really wants to deny themselves and seek first God's kingdom? We like the idea of caring for the poor, but how many of us are willing to actually sacrifice our shelter, money, and food so that someone else won't have to suffer?

Following Jesus is incredibly countercultural. Though we read about, talk about, and worship Jesus, it's fairly rare to find a person who is actually following Jesus in a significant way. And when we do find that person, how many of us try to talk that person out of his or her convictions? Rather than thinking about people in general, stop and consider your own life. As a Christian, you claim to be a follower of Christ. Have you ever thought about what that means?

1. Looking at your life to this point, how well would you say you've done at following Jesus? Why do you say that?

I'm not trying to make you feel guilty for being imperfect. And I'm certainly not suggesting that any of us will be exactly like Jesus in this life. That won't happen until Jesus returns (Philippians 1:6). But being like Jesus needs to be our goal, and following Him is the path to get there.

At this point, you might be convinced. Maybe you initially set out to follow Jesus but got tired or distracted along the way. Maybe you're discouraged because every time you've set out to follow Him, you've failed for one reason or another (we'll talk more about that in the next session). Or maybe you've never stopped to consider which direction you're headed. In all the busyness of planning and maintaining your life, maybe you've never thought about who or what you want to follow.

2. For this question, don't worry about specifics. Would you say that following Jesus has been a consideration in how you have set up or oriented your life? Why or why not?

Regardless of where you are in your walk with God, you have to ask yourself whether or not you really want to follow Jesus—to do what He does and to go where He goes. Maybe even to change the direction of your life altogether. You might think that stopping to consider whether or not you want to follow is unspiritual. But Jesus wants you to think about it. He was very clear about the cost of following Him, and though

He called the disciples to follow Him, He also told them to stop and count the cost.

3. Read Luke 14:25–30. As you read it, take Jesus' words seriously. Consider the very basic statements that Jesus makes. Try to picture yourself in that setting. As you carefully read this passage, ask yourself whether or not you're prepared to accept the cost of following Him. Think about what following Him has cost other people. When you've read and thought about the passage, come back and work through the rest of this session.

Who would start a building project without first considering whether or not they were committed to following through and accepting the cost? Not many would engage in such folly. With this clear analogy, Jesus' statement hits us full force. If you wouldn't build without first calculating the cost, why would you blindly say, "I'm going to follow Jesus" without considering what that really means?

4. Take some time to consider the cost. Don't rush this. If you really began to follow Jesus in every area of your life, what (or who) would it cost you?

In many ways, the concept of following Jesus would have been much easier for the disciples to grasp. Jesus said, "Follow me," and they set down their nets, boats, and families and literally followed Him. When Jesus taught, they listened. When He traveled to the next town, they went with Him. They didn't have to wonder what Jesus would do in a specific situation because they could see what He was doing in every situation.

5. Try to picture yourself as one of the disciples. What would it have been like to literally follow Jesus around, to witness firsthand all of the miraculous, inspiring, and controversial events in His life?

Inevitably, thinking about what it would be like to follow a physical Jesus around leads us to wish that Jesus were standing here next to us. But that's really not the solution to our problem. We'll discuss this more in a later session, but Jesus told His disciples that it would actually be better for them when He left because then the Holy Spirit could come (John 16:7). We may think we're at a disadvantage, but Jesus has left us with everything we need to follow Him in our modern world.

It's important to move beyond the theoretical and think about how this should play out in your everyday life. While following Jesus will include changing many behaviors and certain activities, very often it will mean doing the same things in a different way. For example, I talk to my wife every day. I can choose to speak harshly toward her, or to put her down, or to try to manipulate her through what I say. Or I can follow Jesus and be gracious, loving, and truthful in what I say. When I run into a rude person—on the road, at work, at home—I can respond with sharp or sarcastic words, or I can choose to follow Jesus and show love, even when the person doesn't seem lovable.

6. Consider a typical day in your life. What would it look like if you actually followed Jesus step by step throughout the course of the day? (Try to be descriptive.)

Not only do we have to count the cost and decide to follow Jesus, but we all have obstacles that we need to overcome as well. My greatest obstacle is myself. Too often, I decide that I'm living for myself, for my comfort, for my glory. I have to constantly remind myself that it's about Jesus—I'm living for His calling, His mission, His glory. But even when I get my head on straight, there are still other obstacles. I get worried about what other people will think. Satan will try to derail me through a wide variety of temptations. Even my own family members can be obstacles if I love and pursue them more than I love and pursue Jesus.

7. No matter who you are, obstacles will try to keep you from truly following Jesus. What (or who) are those obstacles in your life?

8. How can you begin to overcome them?

w/ the help of the HS

how can we help each other?
— count the cost
— overcome obstacles
— live for Jesus

Again, following Jesus is countercultural. As Jesus was traveling with His disciples, a person came up to Him and said, "I will follow you wherever you go." Jesus' reply was simple: "Foxes have holes, and birds of the air have nests, but the Son of Man has nowhere to lay his head" (Luke 9:57–58). Jesus' call to count the cost is important. When we follow Jesus, He will very often lead us down narrow paths that are not very popular. But if we count the cost before we start, then it doesn't matter what we encounter because we know He is worth it.

9. Without a doubt, if you begin to truly live like Jesus, you will look strange to the people around you. How do you think people will respond to you? What do you think they will say or do?

When I try to follow Jesus in ways that don't come naturally to me, I quickly learn that simply trying harder doesn't get me where I need to go. Maybe you're a naturally kind and truthful person, but it's agony for you to boldly represent Christ among people who think Christianity is stupid. Or maybe manipulation and put-down remarks are longtime habits for you, and when you seriously try to clean up those problems, you fail over and over.

In HOLY SPIRIT Sessions 1 and 2 we will begin to deal with the question "So what do I do when trying harder doesn't work?" But the answers to that question won't get us anywhere until we settle the issue of commitment and surrender. How badly do you want to learn to follow Jesus? Are you all in, or are you taking a wait-and-see approach? Are you willing to surrender, to let Jesus tell you what to do?

10. Where are you right now on the question of commitment and surrender to following Jesus? Have you counted the cost and decided to commit? Are there concerns or sins that hold you back from surrender? If so, what are they?

Jesus told His disciples outright, "Apart from me you can do nothing" (John 15:5). The call to follow is clear, and the concept is simple. But don't think that it will be easy, at least not in human terms. But what is impossible for man is possible for God.

The most important way that God enables us to follow Jesus is through the Holy Spirit. We will talk more about Him in HOLY SPIRIT Sessions 1 and 2, but it's essential that we not think about following Jesus without relying on the power of the Spirit. In addition, God has placed each of us within a group of believers so that we can help each other to follow Jesus more fully. (Future BASIC films will focus on what it means for us to live as the church.)

For now, begin by praying that God will fill you with His Spirit, challenge you to follow Jesus, and provide the strength and wisdom that you will need in order to follow Jesus. When we pray, we declare our need for God. In prayer, we come honestly before God, admitting that we have failed to follow Jesus as we ought and asking for strength to continue. And this is exactly the type of prayer that God promises to answer: "This is the confidence that we have toward him, that if we ask anything according to his will he hears us. And if we know that he hears us in whatever we ask, we know that we have the requests that we have asked of him" (1 John 5:14–15).

11. Spend some time in prayer. Ask God to give you a childlike faith that believes and follows Him with simplicity and confidence. Pray that God will help you to overcome the obstacles and begin to follow Him immediately.

FOLLOW JESUS
Session 2

Following Jesus in the midst of our modern world can be difficult. So much distracts us from seeing what this life is really about. In our fast-paced technology-dependent society, we have trouble relating to the world of Jesus and His disciples. When I think about the concept of "following Jesus," I sometimes picture dusty roads, sandals, and robes rather than freeways, shopping malls, and wireless Internet. That phrasing may seem a bit silly, but it's so important that when we read about people following Jesus in the first century, we understand what that means for us in the twenty-first century.

1. While it's always been difficult to follow Jesus, what are some of the unique challenges that come from living in our modern world? How do these challenges affect you?

In the last session, we focused on counting the cost. In this session, I want to make the cost and the rewards of following Jesus more vivid by walking through this process with the disciples. In Mark 10, the disciples were with Jesus as the so-called "Rich Young Ruler" came seeking eternal life (Matthew lets us know that the man was young, and Luke notes that he was a ruler of some sort). This event had a big impact on the disciples. When Jesus had first called them to follow, they had left everything behind and had gone wherever Jesus went. As Jesus healed the sick, cast out demons, and taught large crowds, the disciples were right there with Him. By this point, they had seen some incredible things. But this interaction with the Rich Young Ruler seems to have caught them off guard. Somehow, Jesus' response to this young man left them "amazed" (v. 24) and "exceedingly astonished" (v. 26).

2. Read Mark 10:17–31. As you read it, try to experience the event. Don't just read over the words, but allow the passage to form a picture in your mind. Pay attention to what each person says and how they respond. Pay attention to the expression on the young man's face as the story unfolds. Watch for Jesus' expression. What tone of voice does He use when He delivers each line of dialogue? After you've spent some time in the passage, then continue below.

3. Even though he lived two thousand years ago, try to place yourself in the shoes of this young ruler. He was politically influential and extremely rich. When Jesus called him to leave all of that behind and follow Him, he walked away sad. Picture yourself in a similar position. Would you have responded differently? Why do you say that?

If we try to overspiritualize a story like this, we run the risk of assuming that leaving everything to follow Jesus should be easy. But both Jesus' words and the disciples' response ground us in reality at this point. After Jesus said, "How difficult it will be for those who have wealth to enter the kingdom of God!" (Mark 10:23), He immediately broadened the statement and repeated Himself: "Children, how difficult it is to enter the kingdom of God!" (v. 24). Jesus recognized that following Him is a sacrifice that most people won't be willing to make. And the disciples echoed Jesus' realism: "Then who can be saved?" (v. 26).

Until we feel the burden of this overwhelming sacrifice, we don't understand what it means to follow Jesus. Until we question our ability to follow, we're really not picking up on what Jesus is saying. The disciples asked Jesus, "Who can be saved?" I would expect Jesus to reply something like, "Don't worry, just do your best," or, "I just want you to be heading in the right direction." But rather than softening the blow and encouraging them at this point, Jesus put the final nail in the coffin: "With man it is impossible" (v. 27).

From the outset we need to understand that we are not able to follow Jesus. We find it difficult to follow Him because it's impossible! Though Jesus calls us to follow Him, He also tells us that He's calling us to do the impossible. That's why He points us outside of ourselves: "With man it is impossible, but not with God. For all things are possible with God" (v. 27). As we set out to follow Jesus, the real question is whose strength are you relying on?

4. Let the force of Jesus' words hit you: "With man it is impossible, but not with God. For all things are possible with God." How should this simple statement change the way you approach the concept of following Jesus?

Again, we can easily overspiritualize these things. Once we recognize that it's impossible for us but possible for God, we might adopt a "let go and let God" mentality. While it's important to stop trying on our own and begin relying on God, we sometimes use a statement like this to justify our inactivity. But for the disciples, following Jesus was anything but abstract. Peter's statement forces us to see the reality of their situation: "See, we have left everything and followed you" (Mark 10:28).

For the disciples, when Jesus called them to do something, they didn't have the luxury of explaining it away. Jesus was there leading them, and they had to choose whether or not they were going to take that next step in

[handwritten: again ... not of ourselves, but by and thru of Him]

following Him. He called them to leave their lives, families, and businesses, and they left everything and followed Him.

So what is Jesus calling you to do? I think that most of us tend to approach this question in a vague, big picture sort of way. Don't think about where Jesus might want you in twenty years. Start by considering the concrete commands that Jesus has given to every one of His followers.

5. I've listed a handful of Jesus' commands below. For each of these, describe what following this command would look like in your everyday life. Don't think about what it would be like to follow these commands in generalities. Describe what it would look like to completely follow each of these commands in your unique life situation.

a. "Love your enemies, do good to those who hate you" (Luke 6:27).

b. "Make disciples of all nations ... teaching them to observe all that I have commanded you" (Matthew 28:19–20).

c. Feed the hungry, show hospitality to strangers, care for the sick, visit those in prison (Matthew 25:35–36).

d. "Do not lay up for yourselves treasures on earth ... but lay up for yourselves treasures in heaven.... You cannot serve God and money" (Matthew 6:19–24).

e. "You shall love your neighbor as yourself" (Matthew 22:39).

Following Jesus is difficult because it involves concrete, real-life situations. It involves every moment of our lives. We can't simply follow Jesus in our minds or in our church services. It has to be played out in the boring details of everyday life. This is why Jesus calls us first to count the cost. When Peter said, "We have left everything and followed you," Jesus didn't try to soften the blow. He didn't minimize their sacrifice—He acknowledged that they had given up houses, siblings, parents, children, and land.

Instead, Jesus' response was both compassionate and beautiful. He pointed them to a deeper reality. We get so caught up in the world as we see it, but Jesus invited them to see the world as it really is. The disciples saw what they had sacrificed, but Jesus pointed them to what they had gained: "Truly, I say to you, there is no one who has left house or brothers or sisters or mother or father or children or lands, for my sake and for the gospel, who will not receive a hundredfold now in this time, houses and brothers and sisters and mothers and children and lands, with persecutions, and in the age to come eternal life" (Mark 10:29–30).

6. Picture yourself as one of the disciples, and hear Jesus' words. Spend a few minutes meditating on the rewards that Jesus offers. How does this strike you? Do you have a difficult time embracing this deeper reality that Jesus points us toward? Why or why not?

As we let go of the lives that we have built for ourselves, Jesus provides us with a life that is so much deeper. True, the bulk of our reward will come in the future, but we also receive blessings now. I'd like to spend the rest of this session focusing on two blessings that God gives us that actually serve as resources to help us in following Jesus.

The first blessing is people. As we set out to follow Jesus, God surrounds us with other people who are on the same journey. You've already discussed some of the benefits of this in your small-group time, but it would be difficult to overestimate the importance of the other Christians in our lives. The disciples were given the impossible task of reaching the world with the message of Jesus. As we read the book of Acts, we see just how important their relationships were in fulfilling this mission.

God has placed specific people around you in order to help you follow Jesus. You may not like everything about those people (you may like almost nothing about them), but you are an essential resource for them, and they are an essential resource for you.

7. Take a minute to think about the Christians God has placed in your life. Don't rush this. How might they be able to help you in the concrete areas we've been considering, like helping those who hate you, caring for the poor, making disciples, and loving your neighbors?

8. How might God use you to help them follow Jesus in those same areas? Do you find yourself talking people down from their convictions? Or are you someone who encourages the believers in your life to follow Jesus down the narrow road?

The other blessing I want to mention here is the Holy Spirit. We will spend the next two sessions discussing Him, but it's important to realize that we simply cannot follow Jesus without the Holy Spirit. He is the one who works within us to change our desires, and He gives us the strength to follow. While our goal in following Jesus is to please God, we have to understand that we are completely dependent upon Him as we follow. Before you walk away from this session, spend some time in prayer. Humbly recognize your desperate need for God. Ask Him to work in your life, to make you a true follower of Jesus.

9. It's not enough to think about what it means to follow Jesus. We need the very Spirit of Jesus, because this is impossible for all of us. But what is impossible for us is possible for God. Spend some time in prayer. Ask Him to change you from the inside out, to remake you into a follower. Ask the Holy Spirit to empower you to live the life God has designed you to live.

1 2 3

HOLY SPIRIT

HOLY SPIRIT
Session 1

When the Holy Spirit came, He changed everything. He took weak, ordinary men and used them to "turn the world upside down" (Acts 17:6). Later in this session, you will read through the account of His coming in Acts 2. But first, it's important to understand the tension and uncertainty that the disciples experienced before being empowered and transformed.

When Jesus left to go to His Father, He left His disciples with an impossible task: Change the world! I can't imagine what it must have been like for the disciples when Jesus gave them this commission. Remember that these disciples were common, uneducated men. They had given up what little they had and spent the last three years of their lives following Jesus from place to place. Having just witnessed Jesus' crucifixion, they knew the difficulties and the dangers of proclaiming the message of the gospel. The disciples thought that Jesus was the Messiah, the one who would come to rescue Israel and be their king. But when Jesus was killed as a common criminal, they became disillusioned.

When Jesus was raised from the dead, however, everything changed. After only three days, what had looked like a complete failure turned out to be a resounding victory. The disciples realized that Jesus was indeed the Messiah, so they asked Him, "Lord, will you at this time restore the kingdom to Israel?" (Acts 1:6). Once again, they were filled with hope that Jesus would fulfill His mission, rescue His people, and bring peace to the whole world.

Imagine their shock, then, when Jesus said, "No, I'm leaving to go back to My Father. I want *you* to go out and change the world." In essence, that's the Great Commission—"Go into all the world and make disciples" (see Matthew 28:19). In response to the disciples' question about whether He would restore the kingdom to Israel, Jesus said, "It is not for you to know times or seasons that the Father has fixed by his own authority. But you will receive power when the Holy Spirit has come upon you, and you will be my witnesses in Jerusalem and in all Judea and Samaria, and to the end of the earth" (Acts 1:7–8).

1. If you're anything like me, you're very confident in Jesus' ability but very skeptical of your own. Try to place yourself in the disciples' shoes. What would it be like to have Jesus tell you that He wants to change the world, and He wants *you* to do it?

Significantly, even while Jesus was telling His disciples to go change the world, He told them that they first had to wait. At the end of Luke, Jesus told them they would be His witnesses, but then He said, "Stay in the city until you are clothed with power from on high" (Luke 24.49). As he began writing the book of Acts, Luke referred back to Jesus' statement: "While staying with them he ordered them not to depart from Jerusalem, but to wait for the promise of the Father, which, he said, 'you heard from me; for John baptized with water, but you will be baptized with the Holy Spirit not many days from now'" (Acts 1:4–5).

So the disciples were given this impossible task of changing the world, but first they had to wait. Jesus was clear that they couldn't even begin to accomplish their mission without the Holy Spirit.

In the last two sessions we've been wrestling with what it looks like to follow Jesus. In some ways, following Jesus is easy because He gives us clear commands to follow: Love your neighbor as yourself, care for the poor, make disciples, etc. But we all know that following Jesus in every circumstance can be difficult. When Jesus sent out His disciples to continue His mission on earth, He told them that they couldn't do it without the Holy Spirit. And the same is true for us—we simply cannot follow Jesus apart from the power of the Holy Spirit.

Unfortunately, we all meet with failure because we try to follow Jesus in our own strength rather than relying on the Spirit's power and guidance. Think about your own experience with seeking to rely on the Spirit of God. Maybe you've never consciously decided to submit to the Holy Spirit. Maybe you have never cried out in prayer for the Spirit's help. Or maybe you're one of those rare people who really does try to live every moment in the power of the Spirit. Whichever way, we all have room to grow, and we all have times when we rely on ourselves rather than the Spirit.

2. Try to honestly evaluate your life. Why don't you rely on the Holy Spirit as
you seek to follow Jesus? Is it because you don't want to give up control?
Is it because you don't know how? Is it because you've tried it before and
failed? Try to be descriptive.

If you're having trouble seeing what it means to live in the power of the
Spirit, you're in good company. I'm sure that the disciples wrestled with a
lot of uncertainty as well. After Jesus had given them this huge task, He told
them to wait for the Holy Spirit. I'm sure they were excited, but they really
didn't know what to expect. Jesus said He would send the Holy Spirit and
they would be "clothed with power from on high." But what does that look
like? When would it happen?

Though the disciples didn't know exactly what the Spirit would do when
He came, one thing is certain: When He showed up, they were all blown
away!

3. Whether we base it on our own experiences, our theological "camp,"
our churches, or whatever, we all hold certain views of how the Holy
Spirit does and doesn't work. Get some of your thoughts on paper. What
are your expectations of how the Spirit might choose to work through
you? Does Scripture back these up? Do you think you should broaden or
let go of these expectations?

4. Read Acts 2. As you read it, try to place yourself in the story. Imagine that you're one of the disciples. Try to feel the loss, victory, and uncertainty that the disciples would have experienced leading up to this point. Don't read too quickly, but allow yourself to picture and contemplate everything that's going on in this passage. When you're done reading the chapter, come back and work through the rest of this session.

5. Imagine being a part of the events in Acts 2. Try to describe what it would have been like to experience those events.

Sometimes we don't experience the Spirit's power in our lives because all we're looking for is a spiritual experience. Don't get me wrong; when the Spirit works through us, it is an incredible experience! But that's really not the point.

When the Spirit arrived, He immediately moved and empowered the disciples to act. They didn't have to ask each other if this was what they had been waiting for—they knew it was, and they immediately did what the Spirit moved them to do. The Spirit does not always move as visibly as He did in Acts 2, but when He leads us to do something, we need to step into action.

6. Too often, we know that the Holy Spirit is prompting us to go somewhere and do something, but we explain it away. Has the Spirit been moving you to do anything? If He did, would you be willing to get up and follow His leading? Why do you say that?

Every time I read Acts 2, I'm blown away by how supernatural the whole thing is. Imagine the disciples trying to plan their ministry outreach for the day of Pentecost: "Okay, we'll start by calling down tongues of fire, then we'll go out and each of us will choose a foreign language to speak in. After we shock everyone with that, then we'll have Peter deliver that sermon he's been working on...."

There's no way the disciples could have planned Pentecost. And that's the point. Jesus has called us to follow Him, He has given us a specific mission and specific commands, and He has sent the Holy Spirit to enable us to do what He calls us to do. The call to follow Jesus and the power of the Spirit go hand in hand. We simply cannot think about following Jesus apart from the

Holy Spirit, and we cannot think about the power of the Spirit apart from actively following Jesus.

As you consider what the power of the Spirit would look like in your life, start by thinking about the commands that Jesus has placed on your life. Jesus calls you to love your neighbor as yourself. You may have absolutely no desire to reach out and love the grouchy person next door. But as you begin to open yourself up to the Holy Spirit, asking Him to give you a heart that loves your neighbor and submitting your plans and desires to Him, He will begin to change you from the inside out. You may not be a naturally loving person, but that's the point: The Spirit works *supernaturally* to accomplish the impossible.

7. For each of the following commands (some of the same commands we considered in FOLLOW JESUS Session 2), describe what following that command would look like in your specific situation. Write down specific people you should reach out to or specific places you should go. After you've made some notes, use this section as a prayer guide. Begin praying every day that God would give you a heart for those people and places.

a. "You shall love your neighbor as yourself" (Matthew 22:39).

b. "Love your enemies, do good to those who hate you" (Luke 6:27).

c. "Make disciples of all nations ... teaching them to observe all that I have commanded you" (Matthew 28:19–20).

d. Feed the hungry, show hospitality to strangers, care for the sick, visit those in prison (Matthew 25:35–36).

In order to follow Jesus in these areas, you will need the Spirit to transform your heart. That's not an easy thing, but it's exactly the kind of thing that the Spirit loves to do. Remember that He is the one who produces the fruit of the Spirit in your life: "love, joy, peace, patience, kindness, goodness, faithfulness, gentleness, self-control" (Gal. 5:22–23), and many others.

As you open up your life to the Spirit, you will begin to see Him working. With every moment of victory and obedience you will know the power He has given you. No longer will you be "quenching the Spirit" in your life (see 1 Thessalonians 5:19). When He came to the disciples in Acts 2, He worked quickly and dramatically. He may do that in your life as well. But be prepared for this process to take time. We want quick results with everything, but learning to have the mind of Christ is a lifelong pursuit.

And though the process of becoming more loving, or more joyful, or more gracious might take a long time, you can count on the results being supernatural. Hearing twelve men speaking in different languages and seeing three thousand people submit their lives to following Jesus would have been pretty miraculous. But when the Spirit changes my desires for money, comfort, and safety into desires to love other people, care for the needy, and make disciples for Jesus, that is a very tangible witness of the work of God in my life.

8. The Holy Spirit is a person. He has His own will and desires. We can't reduce Him to a formula or anticipate what He will do in and through us once we submit our lives to Him. The place to begin is prayer. Submit your life to His will. Ask for His power to transform you and to work through you. Confess the areas of your life that you've been holding back for

yourself and ask Him to strengthen and lead you. We will discuss this more in the next session, but start by inviting Him to work in your life in surprising ways.

HOLY SPIRIT
Session 2

Living your life in the power of the Holy Spirit is as easy as walking. For most of us, walking is a simple yet essential part of our everyday lives. We don't think about it, but we depend on walking to make it through our day. And for most of us, walking is easy.

But walking isn't easy for a toddler. It's fun to watch a child learning to walk. She first has to figure out how to stand, which is usually difficult for the child and comical for the parents. Once she can stand on her own, she tries taking a step. Sometimes she'll nail it and remain standing. But usually that one step is enough to make her fall. After a while, that one step turns into two or three wobbly steps. With much effort and a lot of practice, the child is finally able to walk, and the door to a whole new world has been opened.

Or consider a person working through intense physical therapy. For a person who, for whatever reason, has to regain his ability to walk, walking is not easy at all. It requires diligent effort. It will likely be frustrating to work so hard at something that used to come so naturally. He will need to retrain his muscles, retrain his sense of balance, and learn how to put one foot in front of the other.

I'm using this extended analogy because Paul refers to living by the Spirit as walking. In Galatians 5, he says, "If we live by the Spirit, let us also walk by the Spirit" (v. 25), and, "Walk by the Spirit, and you will not gratify the desires of the flesh" (v. 16).

I love that phrase: "Walk by the Spirit." It's so descriptive. Walking is all about motion. It's about heading in a certain direction. Walking is measured not in miles, but in steps. By definition, walking takes place one step at a time.

1. In Galatians 5, Paul uses the phrases "walk by the Spirit" and "be led by the Spirit" interchangeably. Take some time to think about what it means to walk by the Spirit. Why would Paul compare being led by the Spirit to walking? How does the concept of walking help you to understand what it means to follow the Spirit? Don't rush this. Meditate on this for a while, then make some notes.

I think we get frustrated with pursuing the Spirit-filled life when we expect everything to change overnight. I find that as I counsel people through various issues, most of them have a pretty good idea of what they ought to be doing. What they find frustrating is that they keep trying to follow Jesus, but they keep failing. The decision to follow Jesus may have been difficult, but making that decision to follow was much easier than actually following moment by moment in their everyday lives. Inevitably, deciding to step out and follow Jesus means that we will fail.

That's why I find the concept of walking by the Spirit so helpful. There's nothing about the term *walking* that suggests speed, style, fluency, or consistency. You just have to put one foot in front of the other. If you stop walking, all you have to do is take another step to get going again. If you fall down, you can keep walking. You just have to get up and take another step. Like a young child learning to walk, walking by the Spirit is something that becomes more natural over time.

When it comes to following the Spirit's leading, we all fail. Maybe you've given the Spirit-filled life a good shot but gave up once you failed. Maybe you even get tense or angry when I talk about relying on the Spirit rather than yourself. You've tried waiting for the Spirit, but you didn't get the results you were looking for.

That's why the concept of walking by the Spirit is so important. It's not a once-for-all decision. You have to set out walking by the Spirit, but you're going to fail. You might begin praying that the Spirit would increase your love and joy, but after a while you forget, and instead you begin to find joy in your circumstances. And when those circumstances turn bad, you might be tempted to think that walking in the Spirit failed. But it wasn't the Spirit who let you down; you just got off track. You started walking in your own strength rather than walking in the Spirit. Just like the person working through intense physical therapy, you need to retrain yourself to walk by the Spirit.

2. Choose an issue in your life that you want to work on. Maybe it's
   having more joy, or being patient with a family member or coworker,
   or a struggle with lust, or anything else that you've made an attempt
   to improve. Think about that issue for a few minutes. What does the
   struggle look like? When have you made progress? When have you
   failed? What do you tend to do when you fail? Would you say you've
   relied on the Spirit in seeking to glorify God with this part of your life?
   Why or why not? After you've given it some thought, make some notes
   below.

Sometimes we jump to easy answers or self-help materials rather than
taking the time and effort to surrender to and rely on the Holy Spirit. You
might even put undue confidence in a resource like BASIC to turn your life
around. Although following the Spirit can be difficult, any time we put our
faith in something other than God, we're going to fail. There is simply no way
to live the Christian life apart from the Holy Spirit.

3. Read Romans 8:1–16. Pay close attention to the essential role that Paul
   attributes to the Holy Spirit. Look for statements that tell you how important the Spirit is, what He does, and how we rely on Him. After you've
   spent some time meditating on this Scripture passage, come back and
   finish the rest of this session.

4. What does Paul mean when he says, "If the Spirit of him who raised Jesus from the dead dwells in you, he who raised Christ Jesus from the dead will also give life to your mortal bodies through his Spirit who dwells in you" (Romans 8:11)?

When you find yourself feeling defeated by sin, it can be difficult to grasp what it looks like for God to give life to your mortal body through His Spirit. Certainly, Paul is not promising us immediate results. Though the Spirit transforms our lives, He rarely does it in a single day. And even when He works quickly, we need to remember that none of us will be perfect until Jesus comes back. Oswald Chambers once wrote, "We cannot save ourselves—God can. But He will not give us character. We have to work out the salvation that God has worked in."

One of the most important things to understand about the Spirit is that He has the power to change us. You won't follow the Spirit's leading in your life unless you believe that He has the power to transform you. If you believe that He can change you, you will continue to look to Him for strength and guidance, no matter how many times you fall. And if the Spirit really has the power to bring us life, then there really isn't anywhere else to look.

5. Spend some time meditating and praying about Paul's statement in Romans 8:9–11. After you've talked to God about this for a while, make

some notes below. Do you really believe that the Spirit can bring life to your dying body? Why or why not?

6. I don't like to give the Devil much attention; but we are warned in Scripture that he is seeking to devour us (1 Peter 5:8). He wants nothing more than for us to feel defeated and useless. What lies has he been feeding you in regard to your identity in Christ? In regard to your ability to overcome any sin and live in step with the Spirit?

Most of us would like to have some sort of formula for following the Spirit. It would be easier to follow "twelve easy steps for living in the power of the Spirit." But that's not how it works. Remember that the Spirit is a Person, not an impersonal force. And because He is a Person, He may lead you in a different way than He leads me. But while the Spirit will choose to work in different ways with each of us, the first step for all of us is to pursue

Him. If you really want to see Him work in your life, you need to ask Him to work. You need to ask Him what He wants you to do. This won't be a onetime thing. We need to be constantly opening up our lives to the Spirit, constantly submitting ourselves to Him.

7. Do some business with God right now. Don't worry about crafting some sort of eloquent prayer. Just ask Him to help you submit your heart to Him. Be honest about your frustrations, doubts, and failures. Use this time to simply open up your life to the Spirit.

When it comes to prayer, most of us are bad listeners. Even when we understand the importance of prayer, we rarely take the time to listen to what God might be telling us. For many people, the idea of listening in prayer sounds silly because we rarely hear an audible voice answering back. But if you're going to seek the Spirit's leading in your life, you're going to need to learn how to listen. If you want to know what your next step ought to be, you'll need to ask the Spirit to lead you and then patiently wait for Him to guide you.

8. Spend some more time in prayer. This time, ask the Spirit what He wants you to do. And once you've asked, take time to listen. If you're not used to this, it will likely be an awkward and difficult thing to do. Most of us

are not comfortable with silence. But wait for Him to lead you. Maybe He
will bring a person to mind. Or maybe a Scripture passage. Or a sin issue
in your life. Whatever it is, spend some time silently listening to what He
might be leading you to do. After you've spent a few minutes like this,
make some notes below.

If you don't feel like you've heard anything from the Lord, don't worry.
It's really not about hearing an audible voice or even feeling something specific. The important thing is that you're beginning to open up your life to the
Spirit. You're asking Him to guide you, and you're trying to be sensitive to
what He might want for you.

Remember that this isn't a science. You're dealing with a Person, not a
force. The Spirit will work in you when and how He wants to. So if you don't
feel like He's leading you in a specific way, don't get frustrated. Keep opening
up your life to Him, and wait patiently for the results. In my life, I sometimes
see the Spirit working powerfully through me as I counsel someone, pray for
someone, or work through a sin issue. But most often, I see the work of the
Spirit as I look back. I see the progress that I've made in a certain area, or I see
what He's done in the life of someone I've been praying for, and I know that
He has been working powerfully, but sometimes gradually.

And as you wait for the Spirit to lead you, don't forget that Jesus has given
you clear commands to follow. Remember that God sent the Spirit to enable

us to follow Jesus. Don't get so consumed in what the Spirit might want you to do that you forget to love your neighbor, care for the poor, and so forth. Be faithful every day in the little things. As you wait for the Spirit to show you the next step, don't forget to follow Jesus. A step in Jesus' footsteps is always a step in the right direction.

9. You've already spent a lot of time in prayer during this session. Rather than praying again at this point, I want to challenge you to start walking. As you have been praying, what has the Spirit been laying on your heart? What is He leading you to do? Whether it's a "small" step like praying for someone, or a "big" step like selling something you own and giving the money away or sharing your faith with a neighbor, it's time to start walking. Don't keep wondering what God may want you to do in the future. Start with what He's placed on your heart right now. And if you're not sure what He wants you to do right now, start with the clear commands of Jesus. But either way, get out and begin walking step by step in the power of the Spirit.

BASIC.LIVING
Final Session

So where do we go from here? You've spent a lot of time thinking, discussing, and praying over the last several weeks. My prayer is that you've seen God as you've never seen Him before. Every Christian needs to be reminded of how great our God is. I don't know why you chose to go through this study, but I know that encountering God will always leave us in a different place than where we started.

In many ways, knowing God is an end in itself. When we are living with a misunderstanding of who God is, what we need most is to know Him better. God is who He is, and we cannot relate to Him properly until we come to Him as He is. Many people live with a conception of God that matches their personality and interests, but it differs greatly from who God actually is. This is not a minor issue. When we misunderstand God, nothing matters more than learning who He truly is and coming to Him on His terms.

As you've watched, thought about, and discussed these three films, my prayer is that you've grown closer to God and that you now have a more accurate picture of who God is.

> 1. Look back over the past several sessions. Don't worry about the other members of your group; use this time to think about how you've changed. Do you see God differently now than when you started? How so? Don't rush this; try to examine your heart. Make some notes below, and if God has shown you more of who He is, take a minute to thank Him for that.

While understanding God is absolutely essential, many of us have a tendency to turn theology into a game. We try to discover and refine every fine point of systematic theology. And we don't stop with the clear statements of Scripture. We like to have opinions about hypothetical matters as well. The Bible tells us that Jesus never sinned, but what we really want to know is whether or not it would have been possible for Jesus to sin. Jesus calls us to go into all the world and preach the gospel to everyone, but we like to argue about whether or not the hypothetical tribesman living in an unknown jungle can be saved if we don't preach the gospel to him.

I'm not trying to downplay the importance of theology; I'm trying to exalt the importance of acting on what we know. When we truly get to know God better, it changes us. A person who sees God as a cuddly genie in the sky will not live in the same way as a person who truly fears God.

So while I want you to have a more accurate picture of who God is, it's essential that your life is consistent with your view of God. If you fear God, does your life reflect that fear? If you are a follower of Jesus, does that mean anything in your everyday life? If you are led and empowered by the Holy Spirit, does your life look any different from someone who doesn't have the Holy Spirit?

2. Once again, think back over the last several sessions. Can you point to any changes in your actions and lifestyle? If so, write down a few examples. If not, spend a minute thinking and praying about why your studying hasn't affected your life, and make a few notes below.

What I really want you to take from this study is a confidence in God. Confidence in God immediately plays itself out in everyday life. Fear is the natural response to a face-to-face encounter with God. But once we realize who our God is, and once we understand His unconditional love for us, that terror turns into confidence. We still fear Him, but it's a fear that drives out all other fears. The fear of the Lord recognizes that He can do anything. It reassures us that God is the only one we need to fear, and He is the only one we need to please.

That confidence in the Lord should mean that you care less and less about what other people think. Make no mistake, if you really set out to do whatever Jesus teaches, to go wherever the Spirit leads because you have a profound fear of the Lord, many Christians are going to think you're weird and extreme. And they won't be afraid to tell you that. I sometimes wonder how long Jesus would last in our churches before we told Him to move on.

It's difficult to rise above the complacency that is common in so many of our churches today. The way to rediscover our calling as the church is not to look at what's popular among Christians in terms of following Jesus. Instead, we should be looking to God, we should listen to what He says in the Bible, and we should be willing to go anywhere and do anything simply because He calls us to do it. We can't redefine Jesus or church or Christianity to better suit our lifestyles. This is His universe, His church, and we are His people.

3. Take a minute to consider your unique setting. I'm not suggesting that every Christian in your life will try to hinder you from following Jesus, but if you really do this thing, you're going to run into opposition. If you are really going to follow wherever the Spirit leads, what will the other Christians around you say? Try to be realistic. How might they try to dissuade or push you toward a more comfortable lifestyle? Make some notes below, then spend a few minutes praying that God will help you count the cost and overcome these obstacles.

A new confidence in the Lord should lead you to do whatever He calls you to do. That's the real point of all of this. James tells us to "be doers of the word, and not hearers only, deceiving yourselves" (James 1:22). If all we do is listen to God's Word, we're just fooling ourselves. The character of God moves us to action. The commands of Jesus demand something of us. The Spirit's guidance pulls us in a specific direction. It's not enough to understand who God is and hear what He says. We need to act.

Most often, action is the hard part. I've tried to be practical in this workbook, but I know that many people are very concrete thinkers. Abstractions are fine, but unless we understand how these things should play out in our lives, we're missing it. So I'll finish this session with some very practical suggestions for how this could play out in your life.

Before we get there, though, I should mention that part of me hesitates to give practical suggestions. I'm afraid that you may feel the conviction of the Holy Spirit, then look to these suggestions as ways to remove the guilt you feel for not doing anything. If you find yourself convicted to follow Jesus and then read from a list that tells you to give some money to the poor, you might be tempted do this one action and conclude that you're following Jesus. Obviously, following Jesus is so much more comprehensive than following a few bullet points.

Following the Spirit can't be about feeling guilty and acting to remove that guilt. In listing the following practical suggestions, my prayer is that you will first seek the Spirit's guidance. What does He want you to do? Remember that the Spirit is a Person, and what may be a good suggestion for me may not be what the Spirit is leading you to do. If you know what the Spirit is calling you to do, then don't waste your time with these suggestions. But if you're stuck on where to begin, use the following suggestions to start on the right track.

If you're going to move forward from here, there are at least a few things that need to be built into your life. I've described three important things below: prayer and meditation, active obedience, and community. Other important things could be included, but these will give you some good places to start. Keep in mind that while these three things are essential, they can look different from one person to the next. I've tried to offer a variety of practical suggestions under each, but those suggestions are by no means comprehensive. Use those suggestions to get yourself thinking about what you can do in your unique context.

Prayer and Meditation

This can sound a bit abstract, but I'm talking about stepping away from distractions, coming into the presence of God, and actively seeking what He wants you to do. And as you seek God in prayer, don't forget to spend time in silence as well. Allow Him to "speak" to you, to guide you, and to comfort you with His presence.

When I say "meditation," I'm not talking about the Eastern concept of emptying your mind. I'm talking about allowing your mind to process God's truth. We're so inclined to stay "productive"—to pick up another book, to get out and do something, etc.—that we rarely allow our minds to soak in God's truth.

You should probably spend time in prayer and meditation on your own, but you can also pursue the Lord in these ways along with other people.

Here are some suggested next steps for building prayer and meditation into your life:

- Take a walk around your block. This sounds basic, but by walking in your neighborhood, you will be keeping yourself alert and reminding yourself of the people around you. As you see neighbors' houses, you will be reminded to pray for them and to ask God what He might want you to do in order to reach out to them.

- Take a hike or trip to get away and pray. You could do this alone or with other people, but getting away from the pressures of your everyday life can be a great way to clear your mind and pursue God without distractions.

- Build a prayer and meditation time into your schedule. We all need to be praying on a regular basis, but there's no formula for how much or how often we need to pray. Paul tells us to simply "pray without ceasing" (1 Thessalonians 5:17). This doesn't mean that we need to be on our knees twenty-four hours a day, but we should have a spirit of prayer, constantly considering God in every decision and in every action. Setting aside a regular prayer time can help to set your mind on pursuing God. And as you spend time in prayer, either by yourself or with a group, listen and meditate. It's important to ask God for things, but don't forget to submit your life to Him and ask Him to lead you.

- Start a prayer group with other Christians or with your family. This could be a great way to build community into your life as well. Having a group that you can pray with can be an excellent way to practice dependence on God.

4. Spend a few minutes seeking God. What might He be calling you to pursue in order to build prayer and meditation into your life? Make some notes below to help you follow up.

Active Obedience

Some Christians have a problem with overactivity, with trying to please God by making sure they're *doing* enough. That's not what I'm advocating. I'm simply calling you to following James' command: Be a doer of the Word, and not a hearer only. If all you do is seek God's will but never act on it, you're really not living in a relationship with God.

Jesus calls you to follow Him, so find some concrete ways that you can get out and act. And be intentional about choosing activities that will take you outside of your comfort zone. You may not know what you're doing, but even if you fail, you're still pursuing the Spirit's leading. There is an amazing fellowship with God that comes through following Him into difficult situations. And if you fail, you still have your community of fellow Christians who can help you work through what went wrong and help get you back on your feet.

Here are some suggested next steps for actively following Jesus:

- If God has been placing people on your heart during this study, call them and ask them to meet you for coffee. Begin or continue a relationship with them that will allow you to serve them in some way.

- Make a list of people who have hurt you and you haven't yet forgiven. Pray through this list, and consider the forgiveness of Christ. For some of the people on the list, you might just need to give them a call and talk about it. For other people, you might want to meet with a mature friend or leader and talk about what to do.

- Find a need within your church that you can start meeting. This could be anything: setting up chairs, greeting people, running sound, playing on the worship team, joining a prayer team, joining an outreach team, visiting people in the hospital, etc.

- Start giving money to your church, to other charitable organizations, or to the poor around you. This isn't about the money itself; it's a way to follow Jesus' call to love your neighbor as yourself. By giving financially, you support the outreach of your church. God has not given you money to make you comfortable but so that you can be a blessing to a hurting world.

- Pray for (and look for) opportunities to share your faith. As you watch for these opportunities, pray for boldness to share even when it's uncomfortable.

5. Spend a few minutes seeking God. What might He be calling you to pursue in order to build active obedience into your life? Make some notes below to help you follow up.

Community

Again, this may be an abstract concept, but I want to use it in a concrete way. By "community" I mean a group of people whom you see face-to-face on a regular basis over a long period of time. These are people who can get to know you, people you can share your life with, people who can encourage, challenge, and guide you as you seek to follow Christ. This doesn't have to look like a typical small group, but we all need these people in our lives. Not only has God designed us to work this way as individuals, but this is also His plan for the church. We need people to be closely involved in our lives.

Here are some suggested next steps for building community into your life:

- Make a commitment to keep meeting with your small group. You could set a time limit (six weeks or so), or you could continue to meet indefinitely. Since you've all been through this study, you can keep challenging each other to live this out.

- Join or start a prayer group. You don't need to work through any sort of Bible study curriculum, just get together with other Christians and pray. For many people, praying side by side with a group is an incredible bonding experience. As you pray for your needs and the needs of the people and communities around you, you will likely find the Spirit using your group to meet many of those needs yourselves.

- Find people in your church that you can minister to. You don't have to prepare a sermon or develop an evangelistic campaign, but some of the best fellowship comes through meeting someone's needs. As you model Christ's love to hurting people in your church, they may begin to act accordingly. This could be a great way to join with other Christians in following Jesus.

- Reach out to the hurting people around you. They could be people in your neighborhood, in your workplace, or wherever. Jesus calls us to make disciples. As you reach out to hurting people with the love of Christ, praying that the Spirit would work in their hearts, you may begin to experience what the disciples ran into in Acts 2, where more people were added to their group on a regular basis.

6. Spend a few minutes seeking God. What might He be calling you to pursue in order to build community into your life? Make some notes below to help you follow up.

As you finish this study, you may still have questions that haven't been sufficiently answered. I encourage you to write these down, and go first before the Lord with them. In your time of prayer and meditation, you may be surprised at how God teaches you and instructs you through His Spirit. It can also be really helpful to sit with another believer and learn from his or her insights. The next set of BASIC films will also guide you through what the church is and how it functions.

7. Before you close this study, spend some time in prayer. By now, you know what you need to pray for. You know what God has placed on your heart, where you have difficulty, and what you're having a hard time letting go of. Pray that this would be more than just a Bible study. Pray that you would be a doer of the Word, and not just a hearer.

Tips for Leaders

A good discussion leader doesn't need to have all the answers. Who has all the answers about following Jesus in the power of the Holy Spirit? Only God. You will probably learn more about following Jesus in the power of the Spirit than anyone in your group, because you will have a chance to practice depending on the Spirit each time you lead.

Discussion Leader's Job Description

Your job is simply to:

- Prepare for each meeting

- Keep the discussion moving so that it doesn't get stuck on one question

- Make sure everyone has a chance to talk and no one dominates

(it is not necessary that every person respond aloud to every question, but everyone should have a chance to do so)

• Bring the discussion back on track if it veers off on a tangent

• Decide when to move on to the next question

• Make sure the discussion remains respectful

Preparing for the Discussion

The discussion questions are on the DVD discs for the three films under the "Session 1" and "Session 2" headings respectively. All of the discussion questions appear on-screen. As you cycle through the questions, video clips from the film will pop up to provide context and reminders. As you come to each question, have someone read it aloud. Likewise, you can have someone read the Bible passage aloud when you get to it.

It's a good idea to review the questions before each meeting. If you can, view the film as well.

It may be helpful to arrange chairs in a U shape around the television so that everyone can see the screen and one another. You'll want to dim the lights in the room somewhat so that the screen is clear, but provide enough light so that people can see one another's faces. (You could darken the room to view the film and then turn on a light for your discussion.)

Also, pray before each meeting for the Spirit's leading. Ask Him to help you sense His guidance as you lead the discussion. The on-screen discussion guide does not provide you with the only right answers to the questions. In some cases the right answer is whatever the Spirit says to your unique group. In other cases some answers are more true to the Bible than others, and if you're not sure your group is on track, you can ask your pastor, do some research on your own, or investigate books on the subject.

Most important of all, spend time praying for your group. You can't talk anyone into fearing God or being filled with the Spirit. Pray that the Spirit of God would fill your lives and do the impossible in and through you. In the book of Acts, the human actors were just ordinary, weak people, but the Holy Spirit accomplished unbelievable things through these ordinary people as they prayed and submitted themselves to following His leading. May that be the case with your group.

Guiding the Discussion

A few ground rules can make the discussion deeper:

- *Confidentiality:* Whatever is said in the group stays in the group. Nothing is to be repeated to those who weren't there.

- *Honesty:* We're not here to impress each other. We're here to grow and to know each other.

- *Respect:* Disagreement is welcome. Disrespect is not.

The discussion should be a conversation among the group members, not a one-on-one with the leader. You can encourage this with statements like, "Thanks, Allison. What does everyone else think?" or "Does anyone have a similar experience, or a different one?"

Don't be afraid of silence—it means group members are thinking about how to answer a question. Trust the Spirit, and wait. Sometimes it's helpful to rephrase the question in your own words. Then wait for others' responses, and avoid jumping in with your own.

Be honest with the members of your group. If you desire to grow and change, you will motivate others to do the same. Be open about areas in which you welcome the group's prayer and support. Allow people to challenge your thinking.

Answers that are true to biblical teaching are important, but the BASIC series is most concerned that people may study God and never *know* Him, never be *changed* by Him. With every session, keep asking yourself and your group: "How should this change us? If we really submitted our lives to God and opened ourselves up to His power, what would He have us do? Where would He have us go?" At the end of the day, it's about following Jesus in the power of the Spirit in order to accomplish what God has placed us on this earth to do. It's about advancing the kingdom of God. It's about His will being done on earth as in heaven.

WE ARE CHURCH

BASIC SERIES
featuring FRANCIS CHAN

BASIC is a seven-part series of short films from Flannel, the award-winning creators of the NOOMA film series. BASIC challenges us to be the church as described in Scripture. What is church? You are church. I am church. *We are church*.

FEAR GOD
FOLLOW JESUS
HOLY SPIRIT
FELLOWSHIP
TEACHING
PRAYER
COMMUNION

BASIC.WHO IS GOD?

FOLLOWER'S GUIDE